Our Little Moon

A Grieving Mother's Story

Written by
Jennifer Nguyen

Copyright © 2025 by Jennifer Nguyen

All rights reserved.
No part of this publication may be reproduced, distributed, or transmitted in any form or by any means, including photocopying, recording, electronic, or mechanical methods, without the prior written permission of the copyright holder, except in the case of brief quotations embodied in critical reviews and certain other noncommercial uses permitted by copyright law.

Written and illustrated by Jennifer Nguyen
Cover art by Jennifer Nguyen

This is a work of creative nonfiction. Names and identifying details may have been changed to protect the privacy of individuals.

For information, inquiries, or permission requests, contact:
Email: ourlittlemoon@outlook.com

Printed in the United States of America
First Edition

ISBNs:
Paperback: 979-8-2701-5773-9
Paperback: 979-8-2603-3055-5
Hardcover: 979-8-2703-0810-0
Hardcover: 979-8-2603-3058-6
Hardcover: 979-8-9936147-0-0

Publisher: Self-published by Jennifer Nguyen

10 9 8 7 6 5 4 3 2 1

To our daughter, Luna.

Our moon, Our light, Our Angel

You'll be forever in our hearts

Table of Contents

AUTHOR'S NOTE: .... *I*

INTRODUCTION .... *III*

———— CHAPTER 1 ———— 1

———— CHAPTER 2 ———— 7

———— CHAPTER 3 ———— 13

———— CHAPTER 4 ———— 21

———— CHAPTER 5 ———— 27

———— CHAPTER 6 ———— 33

———— CHAPTER 7 ———— 47

———— CHAPTER 8 ———— 57

———— CHAPTER 9 ———— 63

———— CHAPTER 10 ———— 69

———— CHAPTER 11 ———— 75

———— CHAPTER 12 ———— 83

────── CHAPTER 13 ──────	89
────── CHAPTER 14 ──────	95
────── CHAPTER 15 ──────	109

A FINAL NOTE TO READERS 113

IN LOVING MEMORY OF LUNA 117

A LETTER TO YOUR BABY 123

Author's Note:

This book was never meant to be written as perfect. It was written as scattered thoughts from the mind of a grieving mother whose heart and mind were not fully there.

I wrote this book in a state of depression, anxiety, and overwhelming grief. Each word is a cry for help, a reflection of memories of what once was, and a part of my own journey toward realization and healing.

Some parts might feel repetitive or disorganized. That is because they are. Grief is messy. So is healing. This is not a story told from a clear mind, but one written through tears, heartbreak, and deep emotion. It is my attempt to make sense of everything.

Introduction

I wrote this book to help me cope with the grief of losing my daughter, Luna. Every page is a way to honor and remember her, a collection of all the things I wanted to say to her, if only I could.

They say writing down your feelings can bring comfort, and writing these words to her has helped me find the peace I have been searching for. I cried for days after losing her, and some days, I still do. Other times, my heart feels just a little lighter, not as heavy as it was on the first or the second day. My pain might never go away, but I have learned to live with the burden.

I want to share Luna's story so that other grieving mothers know they are not alone. I hope readers will find comfort in knowing they do not have to suffer in silence, because there is another mother out there who understands what it feels like to lose a child you were so ready to welcome into the world.

Chapter 1

An Answered Prayer

It was late in March,
when the nausea started.

Mommy began having the strongest food cravings,
which was strange,
because cravings like that were rare for her.

She wanted everything.
Whatever she asked for,
Daddy went out and got it for her.
No questions asked.

But Mommy could not shake the feeling
that something was different.
Something deep inside her whispered to look closer,
as if your tiny soul was already reaching out,
letting her know you were there.

So, she took a pregnancy test
and waited.

And there they were—
two pink lines.

In that moment, Mommy forgot how to breathe.
She was startled.
Astonished.
In disbelief.

Did you know, my little moon,
that Mommy and Daddy had always wanted a baby?

We tried for years,
but every test came back negative.
Eventually, Mommy lost hope.
We even started talking about IVF.

So, when those two little lines appeared,
Mommy could hardly believe it.
She was delighted,
but cautious too.

She wondered if it was real.
Could a test be wrong?
Were her eyes playing tricks on her?
Because she could have sworn there were two pink lines.
The second was faint,
but it was there.

To be sure, Mommy made an appointment at the hospital
for a blood test.
She didn't want to give Daddy false hope.
She had to be certain.

Several hours passed,
and then, like a dream come true,
the blood test came back positive.

You were really there.
Mommy couldn't believe it.

No words could ever describe
what she felt in that moment.

You were there,
growing inside her,
a tiny spark of life
that changed everything.

When Mommy showed Daddy the test,
we were both overwhelmed with joy.
Daddy couldn't believe it either.

With just two small lines,
our lives had changed forever.

God had answered our prayer.
You were the gift He gave us,
a blessing,
the start of a new beginning.

Chapter 2

Because You Were Our Moon

When you were around ten weeks,
the doctor asked Mommy to take a genetic blood test.
We were told it could also reveal your gender.

Mommy couldn't wait to know.
We didn't plan a big reveal party,
like most families do.
We didn't want one.
We just wanted to know more about you,
the little life growing quietly inside me.

It didn't matter if you were a boy or a girl.
We would have loved you just the same.
But curiosity has a way of tugging at the heart,
and Mommy wanted to see the face behind the miracle.

No one warned me how much blood they would take.
Eleven tubes.
Just for one test.
Shocking, right?

Mommy had never seen so much blood drawn at once.
I watched as they filled, one by one,
and all I could think was,
I would give it all for you.

For you, Mommy would have done anything.
Anything for her little moon.

When the results came back,
Mommy couldn't wait to see.

She opened the report,
and there it was, written so simply,
yet it changed everything.

It read that, due to the absence of a Y chromosome,
they believed you were a girl.

A baby girl.

My heart lifted in a way I will never forget.
Mommy and Daddy were overjoyed.
We had always dreamed of having a daughter.

Daddy once told me,
"If we ever have a child,
I want a daughter who looks just like you,
my beautiful, loving wife."

And now, here you were,
our dream made real.

So you can imagine how excited your daddy was.
He got his little girl.

You were already loved beyond measure.

Right away,
Mommy and Daddy began searching for the perfect name.

At first, it was hard.
There were so many names to choose from.
We wanted something different and uncommon,
but also simple enough for your grandma to pronounce.

English isn't her first language,
and did you know there are thousands of names?
How do parents ever choose when there are so many?

Mommy and Daddy spent hours searching for a name
that would fit you perfectly,
but we couldn't decide on any.

Eventually, Daddy took the mission to work.
He and his coworker continued the name hunt without Mommy,
determined to find something special,
something beautiful, unique,
and safe from teasing.

Daddy didn't want kids to ever be mean to you because of your name.
He wanted to protect you,
even before you were born.

He and his coworker laughed and joked through countless options.
Every time Daddy found a name he liked,
he would text it to Mommy.

At first, Mommy didn't love any of them.
They were too common,
too plain,
too ordinary.

Then he found it.
He sent Mommy a message.
One word.
One name.

JENNIFER NGUYEN

Luna.

It means moon.

*And in that instant, everything fell into place.
You were meant to be born on Halloween,
under a sky lit by stars and moonlight,
where the night was celebrated by adults and children alike.*

*You were meant to be a child of the night,
a light that would shine forever in our hearts.*

*The name was perfect.
Simple.
Meaningful.
Beautiful.*

*There is a saying,
You are my sun, my moon, and my stars.*

*Mommy loved that saying.
It felt right,
because you were our moon,
our lunar light in the dark,
a gentle glow that filled our hearts with warmth,
a warmth I did not even know existed until you came into our lives.*

*You were ours.
Our little moon.*

*The name Luna reminded Daddy of his own,
four letters,
just like his.*

*So he asked if your middle name could be Mommy's,
so that your full name would carry a piece of us both.*

*A name made from love.
A name made for you.*

*Our bright and shining moon.
Our Luna.*

Chapter 3

Your First Hello

T hey say that with the first pregnancy,
mothers don't usually feel their baby until much later.
One of Mommy's coworkers even told her
that she didn't feel her first baby
until she was at least six months pregnant.

But you were different.
You were so active.
You loved to remind Mommy you were here.

Even in the earliest weeks of her pregnancy.
Mommy remembers the first time she felt you move.

She was sixteen weeks pregnant,
sitting at a red light on the way to the hospital for a blood draw.
It happened so suddenly.
Just a tiny tap.
A tiny little tap.
Barely noticeable.

But Mommy felt it.
She froze for a moment, unsure at first.
Then you kicked again.
And again.

Little taps,
like fluttering wings inside her tummy,
as if you were saying,
"Hello."

As you grew,
your kicks grew stronger.
Mommy could feel you more and more each day.

You would kick her after a meal,
when she went for a walk,
even when she rested.
You kicked and kicked,
as if to say,
"I am here, Mommy."

Whenever Mommy felt your little kick,
she would run to Daddy,
so excited to tell him how strong you were.

Daddy would place his hand on Mommy's tummy
and kiss it gently,
whispering softly that he loved you,
his little moon.

He was so proud of you.
You weren't even born yet,
yet you made us so happy
with your tiny little kicks.

You had such powerful kicks for someone so small,
and you loved to kick Mommy.

But Mommy didn't mind.
She cherished every single one,
waiting for the moment she could finally see the tiny feet
that were dancing inside her tummy.

*Nothing made Mommy happier
than feeling your kicks,
knowing you were there.
Alive.
And well.*

Chapter 4

The Baby Shower

After your twenty-week ultrasound,
when Mommy and Daddy thought
you were safe and sound,

we spread the word far and wide,
sharing our joy,
full of pride.

It finally felt real, like we could breathe.
After so many weeks of worry,
the doctor said you were healthy,
with a strong heartbeat.
No abnormalities.

So we thought we were safe.
The chances of losing you were low,
or so they said.
We were hopeful,
relieved.

And so, we wanted the world to know you were coming.
We told family,
friends,
and coworkers,
everyone who knew us.

They were so excited to meet you.
Some even bought you gifts
before Mommy and Daddy could officially announce the baby shower.

Daddy's mother, your grandma, was the most excited of all.
You were going to be her first and only grandchild.
She had waited a long time for you,
just like Mommy and Daddy.
All her siblings already had grandchildren,
but she had none.
She was so lonely,
so envious.

Grandma wanted a grandchild so badly.
So when we told her the news,
she broke down in tears.

Finally,
God had blessed her.
God had blessed us all.
You were our miracle.

Grandma asked to host the baby shower at her home.
For the first time in years,
she finally had something to celebrate.

There was so much to plan,
but Mommy and Daddy didn't mind.
We wanted this day to be special
for our baby girl.

We picked your theme:

Space.

Full of stars,
planets,
and moons.

Like you,
our little moon.

Your aunt, your daddy's younger sister,
even made you a flyer with the words,
"We are over the Moon."
Because we truly were.

Countless texts were exchanged,
planning your baby shower.
We wanted everything to be perfect.

Everything was chosen with care.
Tablecloths were pink,
decorated with little astronauts floating through space.
Mommy could picture that little astronaut as you,

Adventurous.
Curious.
Brave.

We bought balloons for the decorations,
a huge balloon arch with little planets
orbiting around.

We even rented a jumper for your cousins,
who we knew you would have loved to play with.

Everything was carefully prepared.

JENNIFER NGUYEN

Piñata.
Cake.
Cupcakes.
All kinds of desserts.

Grandma wanted to bake the world for you
and cook enough food to feed an entire country.

Daddy even thought about getting a cotton candy machine.

We wanted to celebrate,
your life,
your arrival,
you.

To the fullest extent.
That is how much we loved you,
our little moon.

Words alone cannot express the joy we felt,
or the anxious excitement
of waiting until we could finally meet you.

We were counting the days,
never knowing how precious each one truly was.

Until that day.

Chapter 5

She Thought She Had Time

J une 29, 2025,
The day that changed everything.

Something was not right.
It began quietly, like a whisper Mommy tried to ignore.
The headaches.
The aches in her body that never truly went away.
Every morning felt heavier than the last.

She told herself it was normal,
that every mother felt this way.
But deep down, she knew something wasn't right.

She had read that headaches could be a sign of preeclampsia.
That word alone terrified her.
Preeclampsia meant she could lose you.
It meant you could be in danger.
The thought was unbearable.

So Mommy wrote to the doctor,
hoping for reassurance,
praying that it wasn't what she feared.

The reply was the same as always,
so carefree,
so simple,
proof that it was all in her mind.
She was overreacting again.

"A headache is not concerning," they said.
"Just take Tylenol and hope it goes away."

So Mommy did.
She swallowed the pills and the fear.
She pushed the worry aside
and told herself she was being dramatic.
She wanted to believe them.
She needed to.

Monday came, and she went to work like always.
The headache faded for a while,
then returned again,
just like the worry she kept forcing away.

Her body ached in strange places.
Her legs were heavy.
Her back screamed with pain.
She told herself it was pregnancy,
that this was how it was supposed to be.

She made tea.
She smiled through the day.
She tried to pretend everything was fine.

And for a little while, it was.
Because she could still feel you move.
Tiny little kicks, soft and sure,
proof that you were there.
Maybe you were.
Were you?

But as the days went by,
each one felt harder than the last.
The exhaustion sank deep into her bones.

Her legs trembled after only a few steps.
It felt like running miles she never took.

Mommy thought about going back to the hospital
to check on you,
but then she remembered the last time,
the way they brushed her off,
their voices calm and certain.

"See? She is fine. The baby is safe."

Maybe she was just overreacting.
Because every time she went before,
you were fine.
You were always fine.

So she told herself the same lie.
You're okay.
I'm okay.
We're okay.

She didn't know then
that this lie would become her greatest regret.

She went to work like normal,
each and every day,
even when her body begged for rest.
Work grew more demanding,
and her back hurt more and more.
Yet she kept going.

The symptoms weren't new.
She had felt them before.

*You were still there,
or so she thought.
There was nothing to worry about.*

*She told herself it was for you.
Mommy had to work.
Mommy and Daddy didn't have the kind of money
that allowed her to stay home.
And to be honest, she wanted to make sure everything was ready
for you,
to ensure you were cared for when you arrived.*

*Because she grew up in a home
where they weren't ready for her.
She grew up with nothing.
So she wanted to make sure you had everything,
everything she never had.*

*She wanted your world to be safe.
She wanted you to be surrounded by warmth,
by love,
by certainty.*

*So we bought it all.
Car seat.
Stroller.
Clothes.
Even storybooks,
so she could read to you before you ever took your first breath.*

*We were ready to welcome you into the world,
my little moon.*

*So working was nothing to Mommy
if it meant taking care of you.
She would go through the pain again and again,
face any suffering
if it meant being able to provide for you in the end.*

*That was all she wanted,
to be able to care for you.*

*So she told herself that over and over again.
Just one more shift.
Just one more day.
Then she would rest.*

*But the last day came,
and exhaustion hit like something she had never felt before.
Her body felt as if it was falling apart.
Still she told herself,
one more day.
One more day.
Then she could rest.*

*Then Saturday arrived,
and finally Mommy was home.
She promised herself she would rest.
You needed rest.
You both did.*

*Because you, who had once been so active,
started to kick less and less each day,
and Mommy couldn't understand why.
Do babies in the womb get tired?*

She wasn't sure.
But she knew she needed rest.

So she did,
or at least she tried.
What she didn't expect
was a phone call from your aunt.
What she didn't know
was that she would one day regret picking up that call.

Your aunt called Mommy with urgent news.
She said Grandma had been in an accident.
Hit by a train.

That was what they told her,
and she panicked.

She was so stressed.
She had never been so stressed.
The headache came rushing back.
The world blurred in that moment.
Had she lost her mother?

They had their differences,
but she didn't want to lose her.
Grandma was her mother, after all.
She couldn't think straight.
Everything felt like it was shattering apart.

But then Daddy came to the rescue.
He didn't believe your aunt,

because your grandmother was known to lie,
and so was your aunt.

He pressed her for answers,
and the truth came out.
There was no accident.
Grandma was perfectly fine.
She just wanted money,
like she always did.

She wanted Mommy to come to her
so she could ask for money again.
That was all it was.
About money.
Not about mommy.
Not about you.
Never about family.
Never about the love she failed to give her own child.

It was always about money.
Always about what she could take
instead of the love a mother should give.

That was why Mommy wanted to be different.
She wanted to give you everything.
The love she never received.
The peace she never had.
The warmth she used to dream about.

She wanted to give you the world,
my little moon.

But her wish never came true.
Because Mommy didn't realize it then,
but that night
she felt you kick again and again.

She didn't know.
She didn't know that it would be the last time she ever felt you.
She didn't know.
How could she have known?

Looking back now, if she had known,
she would have cherished that moment more.
She would have given anything to go back to that night,
to feel your kicks again.

Because what came after
was something she never expected.

When Sunday came,
you didn't move.
She thought you were still there.
She believed you were.

She rested the entire day.
Her headache was gone.
Everything seemed fine.
But something in the back of her mind
kept whispering that it wasn't.
She didn't know why,
but something felt wrong.

And she ignored it,
telling herself she was overreacting.
And that would be another regret Mommy would live with.

Because all the signs were there.
Mommy just chose not to see them.

Even your cat sister,
who never liked to cuddle,
suddenly curled up on her tummy.
Mommy tried to move her,
but she was persistent.
She didn't want to leave your side.
She knew.
Mommy didn't.

She stayed with you all night,
maybe her way of telling you
that she was there.

When the next day came,
Mommy went back to work.
But she didn't feel you.
Not even once.
Not during breakfast,
when you usually kicked.
Not during the walk.
Not after her nap.
Not a single kick.

All the signs were there.
How could she have missed it?

*And yet, Mommy didn't think much of it.
She thought you had shifted position.
They said you were still small,
and that kicks weren't always counted so early.*

*So she didn't worry.
She waited all day,
hoping to feel those little kicks she loved so much.
They never came.
Not even once.*

*That was when Mommy started to panic.
She texted Daddy.*

"I can't feel her."

*But Daddy reassured her it was fine.
Maybe you were just sleeping.
Mommy worked odd hours, after all.
So she tried to stay calm.*

*But when Tuesday came
and you still hadn't moved,
she grew restless.*

*She tried everything.
She drank sugary drinks to wake you up.
She drank cold water.
Anything to feel that kick one last time.
But nothing happened.*

*The lack of movement put her on edge.
She searched for answers,*

telling herself maybe it was all in her head.
It had to be.
Because the truth
was something she couldn't face.

Mommy searched the internet for reasons,
trying to understand why she couldn't feel your kicks.
And just as she hoped,
the internet said movement could be harder to detect at your size.

So Mommy told herself not to panic.
Your twenty-four-week ultrasound was scheduled for that Friday morning.
She would see you then.
You would be okay.

She was just being overprotective,
like a mother should be.
You were fine.
You were fine.

That was what Mommy kept telling herself.

As she waited for that day,
the day she thought would prove you were okay,
she thought she could wait.

But she thought wrong.
She was so wrong.

Chapter 6

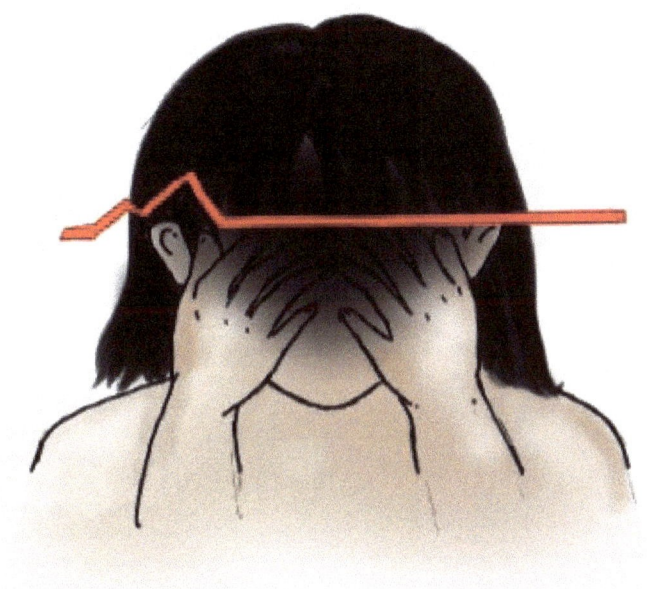

The Stillness That Broke Us

July 11, 2025.
The Friday morning that shattered my world.

Your twenty-four-week ultrasound had finally come.
The wait was over.
Mommy could finally see you again, to prove to herself it was all in her head.

Mommy was nervous,
the kind of nervous that sits deep inside your bones,
when you feel something is terribly wrong
but cannot explain why.

I didn't tell your daddy how scared I was.
I didn't want to make him worry too.
What if it really was just in my head?
What if everything was fine, and you were only resting?

I cannot tell you how many times I begged you to move,
how many times I prayed you were still there.
You hadn't kicked in days.
No sign of movement.
You were always so active, so full of life.
And now there was nothing.

When morning came,
I woke Daddy so we could make it to the appointment.
I told myself that seeing you again would calm the storm inside me,
that once I saw your little heartbeat,
everything would make sense again.

On the way there, I kept touching my belly, silently praying you were fine.
I begged you to move again,
to show me it was all in my mind.

Please move, my baby.
I never wanted anything more in my life.
Just one movement.
Just once.

But you never answered me.
All my prayers fell silent.

At the clinic, we checked in at the desk.
The midwife called Mommy in, weighed her, and went through the usual steps.
Everything felt painfully ordinary,
as if the heaviness in my heart were nothing but an illusion.
As if the world hadn't already begun to tilt.

Then we were led into the room,
the room where we had seen you so many times before.
The room I used to look forward to.
The room that used to make me so happy.
The room where I once laughed at how stubborn you were when you turned away from the ultrasound wand.

Because, my daughter,
you were so shy.
We spent an hour at your twenty-week ultrasound just to see your face.

That room was once filled with happy memories.
It was never the same again after that day.

As always, Daddy was excited.
He had been there for every ultrasound, delighted to watch you grow,
just as Mommy had.
You were his baby girl,
his first child.
He had waited his whole life for you.
We both had.

Like every appointment before,
he took a picture of Mommy and you as we waited,
so we could build memories,
so we could share them with you when you were older.

It never crossed our minds that we might never get that chance.
Not once.

The room was silent,
yet in my mind, I could hear the clock.
Tick.
Tock.
Tick.
Tock.
Each imagined beat echoed louder than the last,
stretching the moment until it felt endless,
as if time itself refused to move forward.

I wanted to tell Daddy how scared I was,
but I couldn't.

*My voice wouldn't come.
My heart was already breaking
from not feeling you all week.
I didn't want to shatter his too.
Not when we didn't yet know for sure.*

*All I could do was pray.
Pray that you were still there.
Pray that it was nothing.*

*Finally, the midwife returned with the ultrasound monitor,
and the scan began.*

*When I looked up at the screen,
I knew.*

*My whole world fell apart.
There was no hope.
All the prayers I had sent felt meaningless.*

*Because there you were—
your tiny body curled face down,
motionless, lifeless.
You weren't moving.*

*I knew.
All the lies I had told myself were just lies.
But I refused to believe it,
because accepting it meant you were gone.*

*It had to be a mistake.
You were sleeping.
You had to be.*

I prayed again and again, begging you to move.

"Please move, Luna."
"Move, my girl."

But lies cannot hide reality when it stares back at you.

Mommy watched as the midwife shook her tummy, trying to wake you.
Nothing.
Not one thump.

You used to have such a strong heartbeat,
like little drums.

Thump.
Thump.
Thump.
Thump.

Now there was only silence.
Pure, unbearable silence.

That silence was louder than anything I had ever heard.
It filled the room.
It filled my lungs.
It filled my heart.

Mommy knew then.
Her worst fear had come true.
Her dream had turned to a nightmare.

And Daddy—
Daddy went completely still.
Your silence broke us both.
No words can describe that ache.
The silence drowned us.

The final blow came when the midwife brought in the Doppler to check for your heartbeat.

Again, there was none.
Not a single heartbeat.

Only a suffocating, soundless reminder
that we would never hear the music of your heart again.

She looked again at the ultrasound.
Still nothing.
No pulse.
No rhythm.
Just stillness.

Your heart wasn't beating.
Your heart had stopped.
And with it, mine.

And just like that,
everything I had ever known collapsed.
All my hopes.
All my dreams.
Shattered by a single missing heartbeat.

I broke.
I screamed.

I cried.
I wanted you.
My baby.
My precious baby.
My little moon.

But your daddy did not scream.
No sobs.
No tears.
Only silence, heavy with despair.

Even through his own pain, he reached for Mommy and held her in his arms.
I saw the look in his eyes as he stared at that ultrasound,
at your tiny body frozen in time,
as if he could somehow fix your heart,
as if our love for you could bring you back.

If only it could.
If only love could solve everything.

He even asked if there was anything we could do to save you.
But there wasn't.
You were already gone.

Chapter 7

The Stranger in the Store

A fter we found out you had passed,
Daddy said he wanted to get rid of all your things.

Everything was still packed in its original boxes,
ready for the day we would bring you home.

But now,
you would never come home.
And Daddy couldn't bear the sight of it.

He told Mommy,
"We have to let it go."

Your things would only remind him of you,
and he was already hurting.

He didn't cry like Mommy,
but deep down inside,
he was falling apart.

He wanted to stay strong for Mommy,
to be her anchor when she was sinking.
He carried an unbearable ache,
a grief too heavy to show.
Yet he hid it,
because he knew Mommy needed him.

He was her rock.
And as they say,
a man doesn't cry.

*So together,
we gathered everything
and set out to return what we could.*

*While waiting in line to return your car seat and stroller,
a kind stranger approached us.*

*He meant no harm.
He thought we were shopping for our baby,
celebrating a joyful moment,
maybe just looking for a better deal.*

*He smiled and said,
"You look like you'll be a mother of three.
You're going to be a great mom."*

*It was meant as an act of kindness,
and Mommy appreciated his words.
She understood his confusion.*

*But it destroyed her—
a haunting reminder of your absence.*

*Because deep down, she already knew.
You weren't coming home.
And she wouldn't get to be
the mother she so desperately wanted to be.*

*Right there, in the store,
Mommy crumbled.
She couldn't hold it in anymore.
Tears streamed down her cheeks
as she struggled to remain steady.*

Daddy gently explained to the man what had happened,
that we had just lost you,
and Mommy was grieving.

The man paused,
then walked over to Daddy and hugged him.

He told us,
"One day, you'll get your miracle.
You'll become parents again."

Because he, too, had lost his children,
and he knew our pain.

He saw us—
our aching hearts,
our quiet despair,
the hopelessness and the shadow of grief
that had swallowed us.

It was in that moment
that your daddy finally let go.

His silence shattered,
and the tears came.

He had tried to be strong,
but losing you was too much,
even for him.

Maybe the stranger was right.
Maybe one day we will be blessed with a child again.
Maybe not.

But if we do, just know this:

*If you ever have siblings,
you will never be replaced.*

*There is only one Luna in our hearts.
And that will always be you,*

our little moon.

Chapter 8

The Longest Wait

July 12, 2025
The Saturday morning that I carried you one last time.

Mommy and Daddy went to the hospital to deliver you.
Empty and broken,
we arrived with heavy hearts.

Daddy held Mommy's hand the whole way there.
Mommy was there in body,
but her heart was gone.
It felt like all the light inside her had faded away.

You were her life.
Without you, the world became a place she no longer recognized.

People smiled as we walked by,
but smiling felt wrong,
like a betrayal to her own heart.

After we checked in,
we were led to our room.
The hospital gave us a quiet room,
far from the other mommies and babies.
They didn't want Mommy's heart to break even more
from hearing their cries.

In the corner stood a bassinet,
the kind where babies are placed after birth.
It broke Mommy's heart to see it there,
because she knew you would never lie in it.

JENNIFER NGUYEN

*This room was supposed to be the place
where Mommy and Daddy greeted you into the world with pride and joy,
where Mommy would first hold you in her arms
while you cried your first cry,
letting everyone know you had arrived.*

*Instead, it became a silent reminder of what could have been.
The prayers Mommy had begged to come true
were now only empty echoes,
lost inside the nightmare
that had become her reality.*

My baby would be born an angel.

*The first nurse greeted us.
She was soft-spoken and kind-hearted.
She did everything she could to make Mommy feel at home.*

*Mommy had so many questions,
but her mind couldn't hold them.
They slipped away like water through her fingers.
Every thought felt distant,
every word too heavy to reach.*

*When the doctor came,
Mommy just stared.
Her lips parted,
but nothing came out.
Her voice was gone,
like the rest of her.*

*It was as if her heart and mind had stopped working together.
She could hear everything around her,
but it all sounded far away,
like she was watching her own life from the outside.*

*The nurse leaned close
and gently reminded Mommy
of the questions she had forgotten.*

*Grief does that.
It empties the mind,
takes away the words,
and leaves only silence,
like drifting in an endless sea with no shore.*

*The nurse stayed near whenever Mommy needed her.
Close by.
Never far.
Quietly present.*

*Before her shift ended,
she hugged Mommy
and cried with us.*

*Then our second nurse came.
She, too, was kind and gentle.
She encouraged Mommy to eat,
but Mommy felt hollow inside.
She couldn't bring herself to touch the food.*

*All she wanted was to weep and to sleep,
and they let her,*

because in her dreams, you were still there.
Still safe within her.

They gave Mommy medicine
to help bring you into the world.
And then we waited.

The longest wait of our lives.
It felt like forever.
Hours that had no end.

Though her heart lay in pieces,
Mommy still held on.
She was waiting to see your little face,
the face she had so often dreamed of.

She needed that moment,
that memory,
to carry with her forever.

CHAPTER 9

Holding You for the First Time

*L*ying there,
  for hours in the hospital,
  Mommy and Daddy watched a movie.
It was the only thing that could keep our minds off you.

But even that was hard.
Every scene blurred together.
Every sound felt distant.

Mommy still hadn't eaten anything,
not since yesterday morning,
the moment she found out
you no longer had a heartbeat.

Her body wanted to fade.
To fade with you.
She wished she could.

Daddy was so worried about Mommy.
He knew she hadn't eaten,
and it broke his heart.

He brought over the hospital food
and tried to feed her himself,
holding the spoon to her lips.
He kept telling her to eat,
but Mommy couldn't.

The sorrow of knowing
you wouldn't be here when she delivered you
was too heavy to bear.

What was the point of eating?
To live?
For a world that had taken you away?

When it was time for the epidural,
Daddy was right there, watching over her.

They missed twice.
Each time they missed, Mommy cried out in pain.
But the pain felt right.
It was something she could feel
when everything else had gone numb.
She welcomed it.

After the epidural finally worked,
Mommy couldn't feel her legs anymore.
Now her body was as numb as her heart.

Daddy helped her shift whenever she was uncomfortable.
He held her hand the whole time,
never once letting go.

He offered her water,
reminding her to stay hydrated,
reminding her that he was there,
because he knew she needed him to be.

Loneliness had never felt so real
until the day Mommy lost you.

Then, around 10:08 p.m.,
the pain returned, fierce and deep.

Mommy knew.
You were coming.

Daddy rushed to call the nurse.
The contractions grew stronger.
The pain grew unbearable.
Her belly hardened,
and a heavy pressure built inside her,
like the world itself was pushing through.

And then she let go.

It was you.
Everything happened so fast.
The nurse called for the doctor,
and they hurried in to help deliver you.

And all mommy could think about was that you were coming into the world in an eternal sleep.

Never knowing how much mommy loved you.

Daddy never let go of Mommy's hand.
Not once.

Mommy took a few deep breaths,
and there you were.
So small.
So still.
So perfect.

At 10:18 p.m., you arrived.
You were twelve and a half inches long
and weighed about five hundred grams.

Lifeless,
but perfect.
My sleeping angel.

Chapter 10

Moonlight and a Father's Love

OUR LITTLE MOON

T he hollow silence
where your cry should have been
was instead filled with agonizing grief,
grief so deep it could not be explained.

Like the night sky without its stars,
vast and empty,
on a cold winter night
without warmth,
only darkness that swallowed everything.

Did you know that everyone in the room cried for you?
The nurses shed tears with us
as we held your small, fragile body close.
You were our precious angel.

Mommy stared at your little face.
You looked so much like your Daddy.
You had his lips, his eyes, his nose.
Your hair was beginning to come in,
and you even had tiny eyebrows
and the faintest little eyelashes.

It was almost ironic.
Everyone thought you would look like Mommy,
but here you were,
a perfect reflection of your Daddy.

Everything about you was his.
And you were perfect.
Just perfect.

The moment Mommy held you in her arms,
it felt like the world stopped spinning.
All the pain she had felt,
all the noise around her,
just faded into silence.

It was only her and you,
like the moon and the night—
always meant to be together,
inseparable even after the moon falls.

There is no night without the moon.

When Mommy finally saw your face,
the face she had dreamed of for so long,
she never wanted to let you go.
She wished that time would stop,
just for a moment,
so you could stay with her forever.

But even that was too much to ask for.

And those feet,
the little feet that had always kicked her from the inside—
she wanted to cherish every part of you.
Every ounce of her being wished
those tiny feet would kick her again.

Your feet were so small,
so delicate.
And your hands,
they had little fingernails,
tiny little fingernails.

*Did you know Mommy always dreamed
of feeling your hand holding hers?
A small grip, so strong, so full of life.*

*And now, she will never feel that grip again,
because you are in your eternal sleep.*

Forever.

*While Mommy was being cleaned up,
Daddy stood by the window with you in his arms.
Mommy watched the way he held you,
so careful, so still,
like you were made of porcelain,
fragile enough to shatter into a million pieces
from the faintest touch.*

There was a full moon shining outside.

*Daddy looked out at the glowing moon,
then down at you.
That was when the tears came—
the ones he had been holding back
so he could take care of Mommy.*

*He whispered,
"That's you, my daughter.
You're our moon.
Whenever we see the moon,
we'll always think of you—
our little moon."*

*Did you know
that around the time you were born,
the moon was at its highest
and brightest point in the sky?*

*It was as if you waited
for the moon to rise
before saying your hello
and your goodbye.*

*As if you were there, high in the sky,
watching over us,
shining your gentle light,
telling us,
"I'm still here.
Don't cry."*

Chapter 11

The Last Goodbye

*T*he night after you arrived,
Mommy slept beside you
all night long.

They placed your tiny body
in a small bassinet next to her bed.
It was close enough
that she could reach out her hand
and touch you whenever she needed to.
And she did.

But even sleep was difficult.
She kept waking up,
her heart racing every time the nurses came
to check your temperature,
to make sure you were kept cold.

She was afraid you would be gone
when she opened her eyes.
She wasn't ready to let you go.
Not yet.

Your little body needed to be kept cool,
they said.
They told Mommy
she could have as much time with you as she needed
before they had to take you away.

But your body was wrapped in ice,
and Mommy could already see
the changes beginning.

*She couldn't bear to watch.
You were still so beautiful, so precious,
but the sight of you fading
was more than her heart could take.*

*It broke her in ways
she didn't know a person could break
until she lost you.*

*Mommy knew she had to let you go,
so they could prepare you
for the ceremony you deserved.
She had to give you back to the hospital,
so they could send you to the mortuary
for your autopsy.*

*She needed to know why.
Why her baby—
who had been so healthy not long ago,
kicking and growing inside her—
was now so silent, so cold,
and so impossibly still beside her.*

*The baby who should have been warm and wiggling,
filling the room with cries,
was quiet.*

*Why?
Why was her baby next to her,
but somehow already so far away?*

*She needed answers.
But answers could never bring you back.*

There were so many things Mommy had to do.
She knew she couldn't keep you forever,
but she wanted to.
She wanted to so badly.

She wanted to bring you home,
to wrap you in a blanket,
to rock you to sleep in her arms.

But that was something
that could never happen.
Not in this lifetime.

So she had to let you go.
And so she did.

Daddy called the nurse
and told her we were ready.

While we waited,
Mommy and Daddy said their final farewell to you,
our moonlight,
our gift from God.

With a trembling voice,
Daddy told you
he would always be there for you.
It didn't matter
that you were born sleeping.
You would forever be a part of him.

He would carry your memory
for the rest of his life.

You weren't just a loss.
You were his.
And he would love you for eternity.

Mommy and Daddy had so many things
they wanted to say,
but our voices were lost
in the weight of grief.
Your silence muted our hearts.

Then the nurse came in
and gently took your tiny body away.

That was when it all felt final.
So painfully real.

Mommy and Daddy held onto your little bassinet,
crying, unable to let go,
staring at the empty space
where you had just been.

The pain was unbearable,
knowing we were about to go home
without you.

Can we still call ourselves parents after this?

We signed the release papers,
packed our bags,
and walked away
from the last moment
we would ever have with you.

*Mommy felt like she left behind
a piece of her heart in that room.*

Chapter 12

Coming Home Without You

Mommy came home
to a quiet house,
a home without a baby in her arms.

She never realized how silent it was
until she came home without you.

All your things had been returned.
There were no signs of you anywhere.
Like you never existed.
Like you were never there.

All she felt now was emptiness.
The spaces you once filled—
now there was nothing.
As if it had all been part of her imagination.

Did she dream of you?

She could still feel your little kicks,
the way her belly would swell with life.

Now it was hollow.
No kicks.
No movement.

Her belly,
once firm with your presence,
was now soft and quiet.

*She closed her eyes
and remembered her moments with you.*

*Late nights in bed,
laughing with Daddy
as her belly moved
while you kicked from within.
You would kick harder
whenever Daddy was near,
as if you knew he was there.*

*You had a favorite song.
Every time Mommy played it,
you would move,
kicking in rhythm,
as if you were dancing.*

*Mommy remembers how you hated Vietnamese food.
She would grow nauseous every time she ate it.
But when she had something sweet,
you would dance with joy.*

*Your favorite was watermelon.
Mommy never loved watermelon so much
until she was pregnant with you.
She once ate a whole one by herself,
just for you.*

*She remembers the moments when she told your Daddy what fruit
you were each week.
The week you were the size of a banana,
Mommy would sing,*

"My little Luna-nana, my little banana,"
and Daddy would laugh.

Now those memories feel like illusions—
just fragments of her imagination.

Did you really exist?
Or was it all a dream?

Her back still ached
from the needle placed during the epidural.
Her body still sore from giving birth.

The pain was real.
But everything else felt like a nightmare,
a loop she could not escape.
An endless weight pressing her down.

The memories of you were too vivid to be imagined,
yet too far to reach.
Was it all real?

She looked at the space
where all your things used to be.
Now it was empty.
Just like her heart.

A black hole filled with broken dreams,
a life without you.

How could she carry on
in a world so dim
without her little moon?

Was that even possible?

What is life without you?

Chapter 13

Joined in Loss. Bound by love

*When Mommy lost you,
all her hopes and dreams vanished too.*

When she first found out she was pregnant with you,
she began dreaming of the life we would have together.

She dreamt of your first word.
Maybe it would have been "Mama."
Maybe "Dada."
She could already picture you as Daddy's little girl.

She dreamt of your first step,
watching you wobble,
terrified you might fall.
She would have cheered you on,
remembering each moment to keep forever.

She dreamt of your first day of school.
How proud she would have been.
Would you make lots of friends?

She dreamt of the playdates,
how you would dress up,
serve tea,
nibble on imaginary food,
and laugh until your cheeks turned pink.
What a wonderful little chef you would have been.

She dreamt of your teenage years,
wondering if she could handle the hormones,
the mood swings.

Would you be difficult?
She would have loved you regardless.

She even dreamt of your wedding,
wondering who could ever be good enough
for her baby girl.
Would he treat you like the princess you were?

But all those dreams came crashing down
in a single day,
in a single moment,
when you were no longer here.

All that remains now
is a trail of broken dreams.
And Mommy couldn't handle it.
She was struggling deep inside.
She didn't know who she was anymore.

Who is she without you?
You gave her a purpose in life.
But now,
what is her purpose?

Your loss was too devastating for her.
She had never felt so alone.
So she reached out to a social media group
for second-trimester pregnancy loss,
hoping to find comfort.

And there,
she found stories much like her own.

OUR LITTLE MOON

Mommy realized she wasn't alone.

Many mothers reached out
to share their own stories,
their sorrow,
their pain.

They understood her grief.

Mommy felt surrounded by love and support
from people she had never met
and might never meet,
yet they cared so deeply.

They offered a safe place,
encouragement,
and understanding.

Their reassurance brought Mommy peace,
knowing she is not alone.

It is hard to understand the feelings of another
unless you have walked the same path—
a connection bonded only
by shared longing,
mourning,
and heartache.

Because of the strength their stories gave Mommy,
Mommy was able to tell yours.
Not because she was healed.
Not because she didn't miss you.

*She loves you too much
to let your story be buried,
forgotten,
lost in time.*

*Your story is meant to be told,
to be carried on,
for eternity.*

*Even long after Mommy is gone,
you will live on—
through this story,*

*forever
and ever.*

Chapter 14

A Mother's Prayer to Another Mother

I t felt like an eternity.
Hours passed.

Many people reached out to Mommy and Daddy,
sending their condolences and support
through texts, social media, and phone calls.

So many words of comfort poured in,
yet none could heal the wound you left behind.

Daddy tried to stay busy, keeping his mind occupied,
while Mommy lay in bed,
recovering from childbirth,
overwhelmed by sorrow.

With only words of comfort
to mend her shattered heart.
But no words in the world
could ever mend a mother's heart
after losing her baby.

She couldn't stop crying.
The tears wouldn't stop.
She hadn't eaten.
Her appetite never returned.

To be honest,
maybe she didn't want to.
Because eating meant she was going to survive
this world without you.

A little part of her didn't want to.
A little part of her wanted to see you.
To hold you again.

Do you know?
Mommy imagines you in her arms all the time.
She can still feel your warm body against her.
She still remembers.

And then there was the guilt.
Her mind kept spinning with what-ifs.

What if she had gone to the doctor sooner,
before the ultrasound?
What if she had fought harder,
demanded more tests, more answers?
What if she had trusted her instincts,
the ones whispering that something was wrong,
even when doctors told her everything was okay?

She should have fought harder.
She trusted too easily.
And now, it felt like betrayal—
not from them, not from the doctors,
but from herself.

Because now you are gone.

If she had done all those things,
would you still be alive?
Would you be here with her now?
Was it her fault?

She had so many regrets,
eating her from the inside.

Her mind became her worst enemy,
flooded with all the possibilities,
all the dreams of you,
all the what-ifs,
all the regrets.

Everything felt so heavy.
Mommy felt so empty,
so broken,
so absolutely destroyed.

Everyone kept telling her she was strong,
that she would survive this.

But she didn't feel strong.
She felt weak,
hollow,
shattered like broken glass.

They told her she needed to get up,
that life would continue on,
dragging her with it.

But what if she didn't want to?
What if she just wanted to pause time,
right where you still exist?

She wondered, why you?
Did she create you so perfectly
that God saw you

JENNIFER NGUYEN

and wanted to keep you in heaven
as an angel by His side?

Mommy grew envious
of all the other mommies out there,
the ones who get to keep their blessings,
while hers is gone.

Everywhere she went,
Mommy kept seeing them.
Babies.
Cute little babies.
Like what you would have been,
if only your heart hadn't stopped.

She knew she shouldn't feel this way,
but it was hard,
knowing she was robbed
of the joy of you.

Social media became a place
of twisted comfort and haunting reality.
Some posts offered condolences,
while others were constant reminders
of all she had lost.

Baby showers.
Newborns.
Other pregnant mommies,
due this year.

Full of joy.
Joy she will never have again.

All she wanted was to scream.
The anger.
The frustration.

Why me?

They blamed her body,
said she failed you
because she couldn't carry you to full term.
And it hurt.
It hurt so badly.

She knew she wasn't supposed to feel this way,
but how could she not,
when she knew
you wouldn't grow alongside those other babies?

She will always be reminded
of what you could have been.

Lying in bed,
drowning in her sorrow,
the grief tugged and pulled her,
like an unseen tide,
sinking her down,
burying her so deep within herself
she didn't have the strength to swim back up.

Sink.
Sink.
Down below,

*where darkness lies,
and no light shines.*

*That was what she wanted to do.
Just sink.*

*The song
"My Daughter, My Love"
by Lyrical Cathedral
played on repeat,
over and over again,
while she dreamed of you.*

*The melody clung to her,
pulling her deeper
into the shadowed pit
of the deep, deep sea.*

*Her eyes were swollen,
red from tears.
Her vision blurred.
Her heart remained torn and bare.*

*She wanted to fade.
Fade away.
It would have been easier
to fade into eternal darkness.
Maybe you would be there with her.*

*Then Daddy came in, holding the phone.
It was Daddy's mother—
your other Grandma.*

She told Mommy to go outside,
to visit the Lady of Peace,
and get some fresh air.
She knew Mommy needed it.

She said if Mommy stayed in bed too long,
she might fall into a deep depression,
a black quicksand with no escape.

And Grandma loved Mommy too much
to let her drown.

She had already lost her granddaughter.
She couldn't bear to lose a daughter-in-law too.

Grandma told her to pray,
that God would heal Mommy.
She just had to believe,
to have faith in Him.

For God has a purpose.
A plan for her.

And so,
Mommy listened.

Mommy and Daddy took your purple box,
the one with all your things from the hospital,
and we went.

When Mommy and Daddy arrived,
we walked straight to the large statue
of the Lady of Peace,

Mother Mary,
a mother who had also lost her son.

Daddy called Grandma,
and we all prayed for you.

With tears in her eyes,
Mommy asked the Lady of Peace
to hold you,
because she couldn't.

You were so far away now.
Mommy couldn't reach you.

The eternal distance,
the one that will forever shatter her heart.

She asked Mother Mary to love you for Mommy,
to tell you that Mommy loves you so, so much.

For Mother Mary was once a mother.
She understands a mother's love.

Mommy didn't want you to think she didn't love you.
She might not have heard your cries,
or comforted you in her arms,
or stayed awake late at night to feed you,
or change your diapers.

But she had loved you every second,
every minute,
every single day
you were in her tummy.

She didn't want you to feel alone up there,
unloved.

Because down here,
you were deeply loved,
by so many.

Your grandma.
Your aunts.
Your uncles.
Your cousins.

They loved you.
They might not have met you in person,
but they loved you.

You might be alone up there right now.
But don't be scared, my daughter.

One day, when her time comes,
Mommy will come find her little moon,
to hold you in her arms again.

Just wait for Mommy.
She will be there.
Just not today.

Not today, because Daddy needs her here with him.
And she cannot abandon him just yet.

So my baby, wait for your Mommy.
She will come for you eventually.

Mommy also asked Mother Mary
to give her and Daddy
the peace they so desperately needed.

For Mother Mary had known
the pain of losing a child.

Daddy and Mommy were so broken.
They will never be the same.

The imprint you left on their hearts
will forever remain.

They pleaded for peace,
to mend their shattered hearts.

We cried under the statue.
Then we went home.

Mommy didn't know why,
but her heart felt a little lighter.

The heaviness began to lift,
like God was helping her carry it.

It was then that Mommy knew:
grief might be too heavy to bear.
The pain might never go away,
forever lingering in the background.

But she can find peace within it.

Grief is like a roller coaster.
It falls.
It twists.
It turns.

Never predictable.
Never gentle.

There will be times when she slips,
deep into the darkness.

But when she does,
her lunar light
will always shine the way for her.

Chapter 15

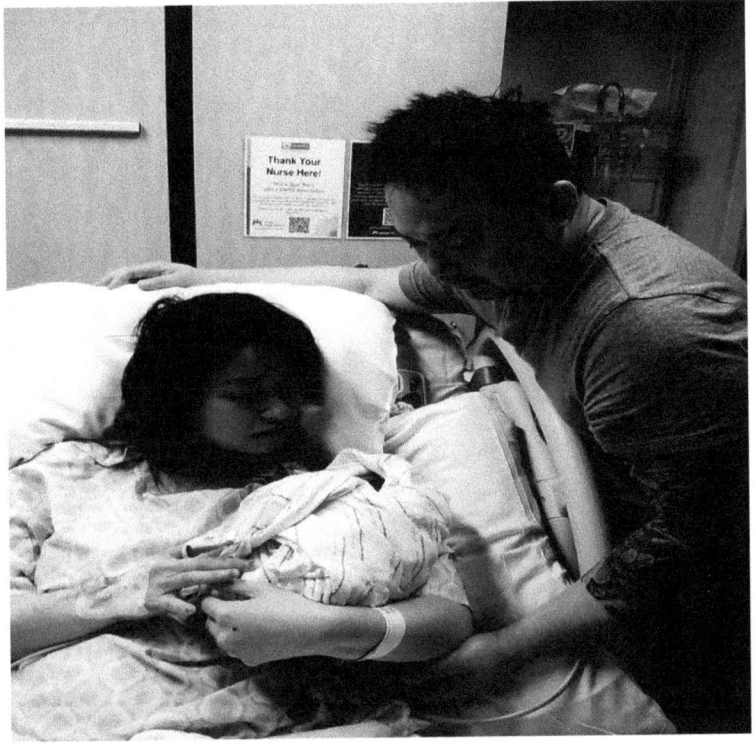

Dear Luna

Dear Luna,

On July 12, 2025, Mommy gave birth to you. You gave me a quick labor, and I am so grateful to you for that. You were kind to me, even in goodbye.

You were the miracle Mommy and Daddy waited so long for, and it pains us deeply to have lost you so soon. I wish I could have held you in my arms and heard you cry. I would have given anything to hear your voice and to see the light in your eyes. There will never be a day that passes when I do not think of you. You will live in my heart forever and ever.

You were my soul, my hope, and my universe. You were the happiness I always longed for. I dreamed of you in that hospital room while your tiny, silent body lay beside mine. I imagined what your face would have looked like if you were alive, how you might have grown, changed, and smiled. Mommy wanted the best for you. I dreamed of your first step, your first word, your reaction to your cat siblings, your first day of school, your graduation, your first love, and your wedding. I just wanted to watch you grow. That is all I ever wanted.

When I was four months pregnant with you, I told Daddy that we had traveled and lived a good life, but something always felt like it was missing. That something was you. You were the missing piece in our lives, but now you are gone before we ever had the chance to feel the full joy of you.

Just know this: I will always miss you. I will keep your photos close to remind me of the beautiful girl who went to heaven to become an angel too soon. I pray that God blesses us again so that we may feel, even just once more, the joy you gave us in such a short time.

I love you forever and ever, my moon. I promise my love for you will never fade, not even in death.

Love always,
Mommy

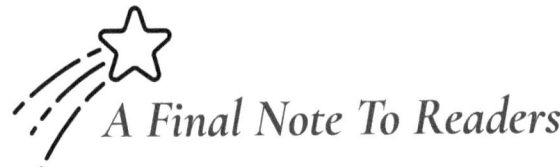

A Final Note To Readers

*I hope this story gave the peace your heart longs for.
No one could prepare us for this,
the heartbreak, the shattered dreams,
the anger, the frustration,
the fear, the trauma, the disappointment that followed.*

*Just know this.
It is okay to feel these emotions.
We are only human, after all.
Grieve how you want to.
How you need to.
There is no correct way.*

*It will not be an easy journey.
It never will be.
We did not just lose our baby.
We lost the future we had planned,
all our hopes and dreams.*

*No parent should ever have to bury their baby.
This cruel world shows no mercy,
forcing us to bear this unimaginable pain.*

*Words cannot express the sorrow we feel.
No one could make it better.
They can only offer words of comfort,
but they cannot erase the pain.*

*Deep down inside,
it will never be enough.
It will not bring them back.
What is lost cannot be changed.*

*We can only find our inner peace within it.
There will be regrets,
moments of what-ifs,
where we will question everything that happened
before and after.*

*We will blame ourselves,
wondering what else we could have done.*

*But please know this:
It is not your fault.*

*Be kind to yourself.
Sometimes the path God chooses for us
is not the one we had in mind.
There was nothing we could have done.*

*The only thing we can do now
is keep their memories alive.*

*Your story matters.
Tell them.
Share them.
Honor them.
Remember their names.
Because they are worth remembering.*

By hearing Luna's story,
I hope her lunar light guides you out of the darkness.
Luna will forever live in my heart,
just as your baby will live in yours.

Their memories will be carried on,
never forgotten,
always cherished.

If no one has told you today,
please remember this.
You are not alone.
You are seen.
You are loved.
And your baby will always be remembered.

Thank you for reading the story of a grieving mother.

In Loving Memory of Luna

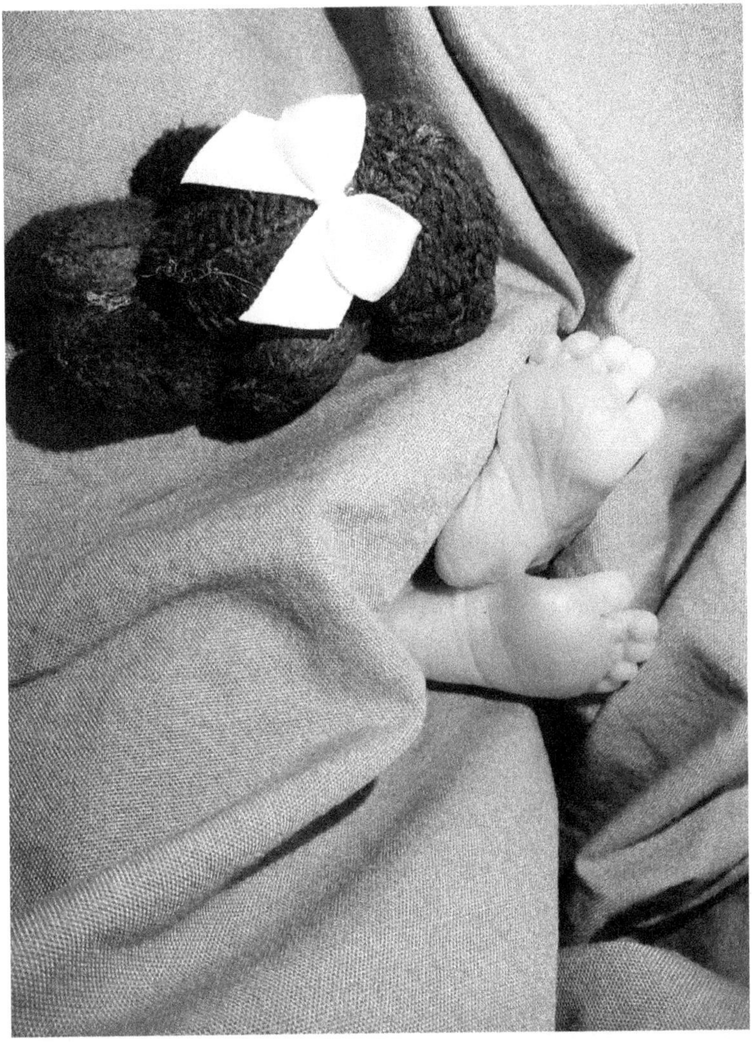

Resources for Grieving Parents:

If you are grieving the loss of your baby, please know that you are not alone.
There are parents who have walked this difficult path and found the peace and comfort they needed to keep going.
Some have even been blessed again with their rainbow babies.

Finding peace does not mean letting go of the memories of your child.
They will forever live within our hearts and souls.
Peace is not forgetting.
It is finding comfort within the pain we carry.

Together, we can find the strength to carry on.

Below are a few organizations and support groups that have helped me and may help you too.

National Organization for Grieving Parents

A nonprofit that provides resources and emotional support for parents who have experienced the loss of a child.
Website: https://www.compassionatefriends.org

Postpartum Support International (PSI)

A virtual support group for parents who have experienced stillbirth or early infant loss.

Offers online sessions, peer support, and access to trained counselors.

Website: https://www.postpartum.net

March of Dimes

A Facebook community offering comfort and encouragement for parents experiencing:

– Preterm birth

– NICU stays

– Infant loss

– Fertility struggles

Search for their online support groups on Facebook or visit: https://www.marchofdimes.org

Second Trimester Pregnancy Loss Support Group (Facebook)

A private Facebook support group for those who have lost a baby during the second trimester.

It offers a safe, understanding space to connect with others who are grieving similar losses.

Search on Facebook: "Second Trimester Pregnancy Loss Support Group"

Sad Dads Club:

Dads, you are not alone. This website was created by three Dads in Maine who have lost their daughters to stillborn, to support other dads who have also lost their child. Offers on their site are virtual meetups and in-person events.

Website: https://saddadsclub.org

Maternal Mental Health Hotline:

For those who need immediate help, this is the National Suicide Prevention Lifeline. The hotline offers interpreter services for over 60 different languages. You can call or text:

883-852-6262

(833)-TCL_MAMA)

A letter to Your Baby

Your story starts here...